THE
CHELMER & BLACKWATER
NAVIGATION

JOHN MARRIAGE

The preserved barge *Susan*, owned by Chelmsford Museum Service, approaches Sandford Lock at full speed, summer 1999. Note the twin rudders mounted on either side of the propellor.

THE
CHELMER & BLACKWATER
NAVIGATION

JOHN MARRIAGE

TEMPUS

First published 2002
Copyright © John Marriage, 2002

Tempus Publishing Limited
The Mill, Brimscombe Port,
Stroud, Gloucestershire, GL5 2QG
www.tempus-publishing.com

ISBN 0 7524 2392 4

Typesetting and origination by
Tempus Publishing Limited
Printed in Great Britain by
Midway Colour Print, Wiltshire

AVIGATION. PAPER·MILLS
BRIDGE. 1927

This copy of a 1927 line drawing depicts the original bridge at Paper Mill Lock designed by
John Rennie in 1793. In the 1930s the bridge was replaced by the present concrete structure.

Contents

AN

A C T

FOR

Making and Maintaining a Navigable Communication between the Town of *Chelmsford*, or some Part of the Parish of *Springfield*, in the County of *Essex*, and a Place called *Collier's Reach*, in or near the River *Blackwater*, in the said County.

𝕎𝕙𝕖𝕣𝕖𝕒𝕤 the making and maintaining of a Preamble. Navigation for the Passage of Boats, Barges, and other Vessels, from or nearly from the Town of *Chelmsford*, or some Part of the Parish of *Springfield*, to or nearly to a Place called *Collier's Reach*, in or near the River *Blackwater*, near the Town and Port of *Maldon*, all in the County of *Essex*, by Means of widening, deepening, cleansing, straightening, and improving the River *Chelmer*, and making Cuts and Deviations by the Sides thereof where necessary, from or nearly from *Chelmsford*, or some Part of the Parish of *Springfield* aforesaid, to a certain Part of the said River, near to *Beleigh Mill*, above the said Town and Port of *Maldon*, and by making a Navigable Cut or Canal from thence into the River *Blackwater*, and by widening, deepening, cleansing, and improving the said River *Blackwater*, and making Cuts and Deviations by the Sides thereof where necessary, to or nearly to a certain Mill called *Heybridge Mill*, and by making a Navigable Cut or Canal from thence, above the said Mill, through the Village of *Heybridge*, to communicate with the said River *Blackwater*, at or nearly at the said

A

The Chelmer Navigation Act of 1793 authorised the widening, deepening and straightening of the River Chelmer plus a small part of the River Blackwater, together with the creation of various navigable cuts. The Act provided a passage for boats between Chelmsford and the Blackwater Estuary and remains completely unchanged on the statute book.

Introduction

At the turn of the eighteenth century Chelmsford, the county town of Essex, was a minor market town straddling the main road from London to Norwich. Most of its bulk imports came by pack mule and heavy cumbersome wagons using the rough turnpike road from the port of Maldon at the head of the long Blackwater estuary. Midway between the two towns, the long drawn-out slope of Danbury Hill intervened. In winter, the route was deeply rutted and muddy, seriously impeding traffic as a result.

Despite the poor state of the road by the 1770s, some 10,000 tons of goods – about half being coal – traversed the Danbury road and it seemed physically impossible for this to be increased further. Elsewhere in Britain there were plans to build canals to transport huge quantities of goods and materials cheaply and efficiently from place to place. Thoughts turned to making the Chelmer – a small river flowing through Chelmsford to the Blackwater estuary – into a navigable waterway, so that bulk goods – particularly coal – could be brought into the town more easily.

In 1677 a scheme was proposed by Andrew Yarranton to make the river navigable but Maldon townsfolk successfully opposed the idea and it was dropped. In 1733 John Hoare, another well-known surveyor, produced two detailed schemes. One suggested fairly conventional improvements to the river, by dredging and building locks, which he estimated would cost about £9,355. The other, a much more radical scheme, envisaged the construction of an entirely new channel along the valley for about £12,870. Both were huge sums at the time and the idea was again shelved. Thirty-two years later enthusiasm had again grown and Thomas Yeoman, a consultant engineer, is reported to have said, 'The utility and benefit of the navigation will first arise from the greater cheapness of carriage. For example, the price of land carriage and all goods brought by wagon from Chelmsford to Maldon is 8/- per ton, whereas tonnage and lighterage by water may be charged at only 2/- per ton. Adding to this a toll of 2/6d, the price will be 4/6d. This will be a saving of nearly half of what each individual pays for each ton of goods by road.'

As a result of his survey, an Act of Parliament was passed in 1766 to make the river navigable from 'the Port of Maldon to the Town of Chelmsford' for boats able to carry 30 tons of cargo. The main wharves and warehouses were to be at Fullbridge, Maldon and Moulsham Bridge, Chelmsford. The Act required the works to be carried out within twelve years but were not allowed to start until the estimated costs of £13,000 had been raised. Sadly, less than half was subscribed and the project again stalled.

All the enthusiasm for the various proposals came from people living in and around Chelmsford, where the benefit would be felt, but fierce opposition continued from Maldonians, who realised – correctly – that they would lose substantial income and jobs derived from tolls, together with harbour and wharfage dues. Allied with them were the millers along the river, who were concerned about the potential loss of water to operate their mill wheels, particularly in times of drought. A leading campaigner against the scheme was John Strutt, a local landowner, whose son was MP for Maldon. However, despite these setbacks, interest in the idea continued and in 1792 a fresh scheme was prepared under the leadership of the ninth Lord Petre of Ingatestone and Thomas Branston, MP of Skreens, Roxwell. To overcome Maldon's opposition, the plans envisaged a new route by passing Maldon by way of a new channel, which would strike the tideway at the highest point of the estuary that heavily laden coal ships could penetrate, without having to unload part of their cargo over the side into lighters.

A basin was proposed at its junction with the estuary, together with a large sea lock, able to take incoming shipping. At the Chelmsford end, a smaller basin was suggested on the north-east side of the town, in Springfield parish rather than in Chelmsford parish where the land was entailed. A short cut was to connect the basin with the river below Moulsham Mill. Costs of this, the most ambitious scheme yet produced, were estimated to be £40,000, with the right to raise a further £20,000 in the form of shares or borrowing on the tolls.

A fresh Act of Parliament was passed in 1793 and named about 150 'proprietors', many of whom, strangely enough, came from Leicestershire. It also specified that the waterway was to be navigable 'for the passage of boats, barges and other vessels'. As was normal in such Acts, a public right to use the canal was included, subject, of course, to the proper payment of tolls. The actual tollages were specified in the Act and ranged from a farthing per mile per quarter for oats, malt and other grain to 2d per chaldron (35 bushels) of coal and 2½d per mile for all other goods. Stone for road making, other than turnpikes (toll roads), was to be carted free. Riparian owner's pleasure craft were also toll free, provided

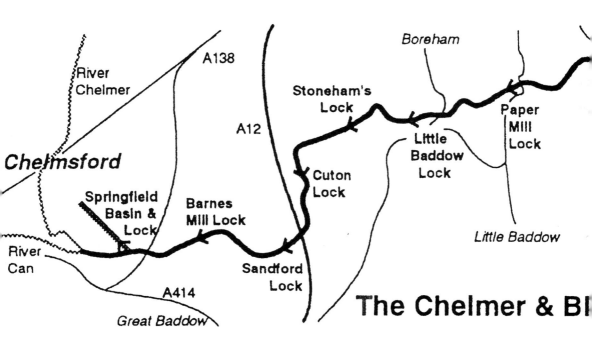

8

the locks were not used. The Act contained powers to compulsorily purchase land and some seventy acres were acquired in this way. Justices of the Peace were empowered to impose transportation to Australia on those found guilty of damage to the Company's property but this has not been invoked for many years! However, other clauses are still applicable and remain important. These include forbidding the obstruction of any part of the navigation by any boat or vessel. Its owner could be fined for every hour the obstruction continued. In addition, the occupier of any mill was held to commit an offence if he permitted the water level on the pound he controlled to fall twenty-one inches below its impounded level. The Company was also required to provide a 'fit and sufficient public wharf with a crane and other engines' next to Springfield Basin.

Although opposition continued, Royal Assent to the Chelmer Navigation Bill was received on 17 June 1793 and remains unchanged on the statute book. It authorised the 'making and maintaining of a navigable communication between the town of Chelmsford, or some part of the parish of Springfield to a place called Colliers's Reach' as mentioned previously. When the news of the Royal Assent reached Chelmsford, cheering crowds gathered in the town and beer was distributed to the people, church bells rang and bonfires lit in the streets, whilst the more well-to-do met for a more genteel celebration in the Black Boy Inn, one of the town's largest and most important coaching inns.

The first meeting of the owners of the proposed navigation – the Company of Proprietors of the Chelmer and Blackwater Navigation Ltd – was held on 15 July 1793 at the Black Boy Hotel, which stood at the junction of Springfield Road and High Street on land now occupied by shops. Construction started later the same year, under the general direction of the famous engineer, John Rennie, F.R.S. (1761-1821), who was responsible for many other contemporary waterways, including the better known Kennet & Avon Canal, where the design of the locks, bridges and other installations are remarkably similar. However, he is reputed to have visited the site only five times and the actual survey of the river was carried out by Charles Wedge. Nevertheless, Rennie kept in close touch with the project via correspondence.

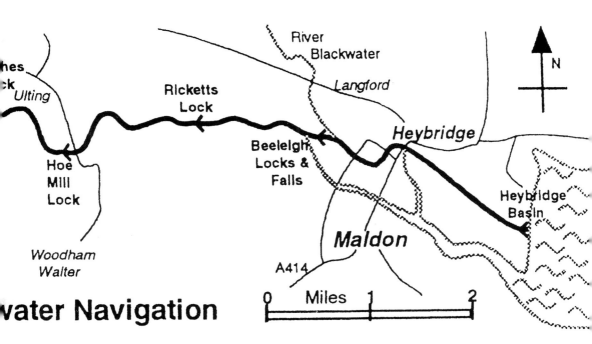

Day-to-day control was vested in the resident engineer, Richard Coates, a Yorkshire man, who immediately prior to this project held a similar position under Rennie to build the Ipswich to Stowmarket Navigation, which it closely resembled. He brought some of his Suffolk navvies, and his brother, George, a stonemason, to carry out the work. Some of the descendants of the former still live at Heybridge Basin, proud of their Suffolk origins.

The total length of the waterway is 13¾ miles. To overcome a fall of over 76ft, twelve locks were built, plus the sea lock at Heybridge Basin, all neatly spaced about one every mile. In addition to the cuts at either end, channels were dug around existing mills and the whole river was widened, straightened and deepened, with wharves built in several places to serve various villages. At 17ft wide and 68ft long the locks could accommodate barges 60ft long by 16ft beam, each able to carry 25 tons of cargo, even though their maximum draft was only 2ft. The sea lock at Heybridge Basin was built to take 300 ton vessels of up to 107ft long by 26ft beam, with a draft of up to 8ft.

It is not known why the particular dimensions of the twelve locks were chosen, but it is possible that they were built to suit lighters already to be found on the estuary. Most of the locks, bridges and lock houses were constructed of bricks made at Sawpit Field, Boreham and Ulting. The locks, bridges and wharves were capped by Dundee Stone, chosen for its hard-wearing qualities and a towpath created from end to end, bridging streams and side channels. A particular feature was the self-closing towpath gates, built as a smaller version of the more common farm gates. They were mounted, in pairs, at an angle to their posts at every field boundary and prevented livestock from straying from field to field, whilst providing an unimpeded route for the barge horses.

On 23 April 1796 the first brig sailed into Heybridge Basin. Its arrival was reported in the *Chelmsford Chronicle* as follows:

> *...there arrived in the grand basin at the entrance to the Chelmer Navigation near Collier's Reach, the good brig* Fortunes Increase, *Robert Parker, master, laden with 150 chaldrons* [just over 5,000 bushels] *of the best Burnmore coals from Sunderland consigned to Messrs Blyth and Coates, the first adventurers on the navigation. This is the first shipload of coal which the navigation has received. It may be worthy of remark that the* Fortunes Increase *is a good old brig and during her journeys on the seas of about forty years has never experienced any misfortune. Yesterday three wagons loaded with coals from a coal yard at Boreham, stocked by the Chelmer Navigation arrived here* [Chelmsford] *with their horses decorated with coloured ribbon as being the first carted coals from that navigation. On Tuesday last* [26 April 1796] *a barge was loaded with nearly 150 sacks of flour at Hoe Mill from where it proceeded by the new navigation to Collier's Reach for the London Market.*

This was the first of many to be carried on the waterway and over a period of time many of the mills were enlarged to take advantage of the easy communications. The navigation was extended in stages to Chelmsford and, in September 1796, two barges loaded with foreign wheat were able to reach Moulsham Mill, just downstream from the town. However, the remainder of the canal was not opened until the middle of the next year.

On 2 June 1797, the *Chelmsford Chronicle* reported that the next day barges loaded with coal would 'proceed in grand procession with colour flying, etc., into the basin near Springfield Bridge, the ground around which is now divided and let to different persons for wharves, will in a few days after the opening be plentifully stored with coals, lime, chalk; cinders [coke], etc.' Not unnaturally, the convoy of boats was met by enthusiastic crowds of townsfolk.

Once opened, the land around was quickly laid out with sawmills, lime kilns, iron foundries, stone masons and coal yards, all served from the water. At the head was a large open wharf and yard area, extending to both Springfield Road and Navigation Road. This was the public wharf as required by the Act. Adjacent, a gas works was built in 1819 (founded by Coates), becoming the first to be built on an inland site in Britain, using coal barged up the navigation. Although the original works have long since disappeared, a gas distribution depot and several gasometers still mark the spot.

On completion of the waterway, Richard Coates became a businessman in Chelmsford and a major carrier on the navigation, eventually to live in a large house near Springfield Basin. In due course the business was taken over by James Brown who, with his son, carried on trading, renaming the firm, Brown & Son. They continued to use the waterway for the carriage of coal, coke, slate and timber. Other users, with their own wharves, included Wells & Perry, coal merchants, Wray & Fuller, stonemasons, and T.D. Ridley & Sons, also coal merchants.

A problem encountered during the construction of the waterway was the existence of a half mile tidal canal leaving the River Chelmer at Beeleigh and terminating at Langford Mill on the River Blackwater. The new waterway sliced through the little canal. After some initial disagreement, the lower section running into the Chelmer was banked off and the upper part was incorporated as a branch of the new navigation, becoming known as Langford Cut, and, until the coming of the railways, was used extensively by Langford Mill for the import of coal and the export of flour.

The early success of the canal prompted the proprietors to consider extensions and Rennie was asked to look into the possibility of making the River Chelmer upstream to Dunmow navigable, and making a branch towards Ongar. However, nothing came of these ideas but, until the railways were built in the 1840s, the waterway carried an immense range of material and goods of all kinds, with coal being the most important. This was delivered to the town and village wharves as well as the millers, who considerably expanded their trade by converting their water wheels to steam power. Somewhat ironically, much of the material used in the construction of the railways was shipped in by the canal. This brief period was the most prosperous in the navigation's history. The completion of the railway from London through Chelmsford to Colchester started a slow decline in the use of water transport, but Brown & Son, timber merchants, continued to import all their foreign soft woods via the waterway, ceasing only in 1972, when the firm was taken over and the trade transferred to road.

When commercial traffic ended, the proprietors decided to open the canal for pleasure traffc of all kinds. They set an example by commissioning the charter barge, *Victoria*. In addition, there are now some 150 motor boats permanently based on the waterway, a similar number of canoes and a small boat hire firm. Nevertheless, the waterway remains the reverse of crowded and has been christened 'Essex's unknown waterway' – in every respect quiet and peaceful.

The seal of the Navigation Company. Its design was inspired by the Naiad Conduit Head which once stood in Tindal Square, Chelmsford. The date commemorates the first meeting of the Company.

One
Springfield Basin

Coates Wharf in 1935, a still active quay used by Brown & Son, timber merchants, who owned and operated their own fleet of horse-drawn barges between Chelmsford and Heybridge Basin.

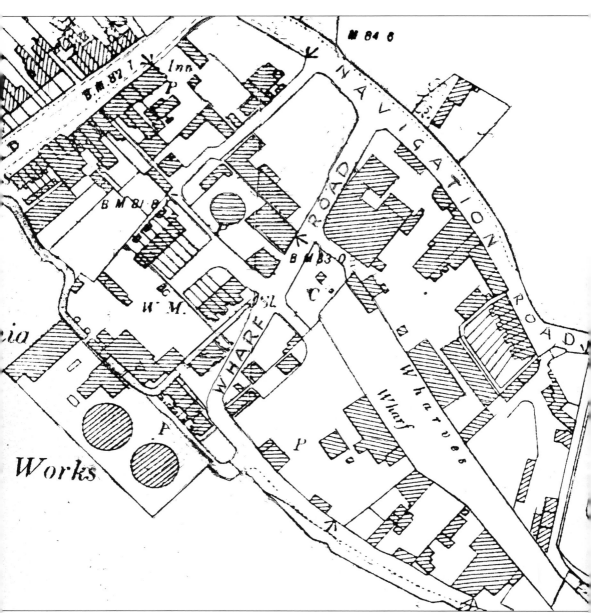

This extract from a 1897 OS map shows Springfield Basin, with industries clustered around. On the north east side, Brown & Son had engulfed the other original users and later expanded further downstream. The public wharf once extended from the head of the basin as far as Springfield Road, but when the map was published it had shrunk to a small piece of land next to Wharf Road. The canal feed can be seen snaking its way towards the waterway from a nearby branch of the River Chelmer.

An aerial view of Springfield Basin, *c*.1935. Brown & Son, occupied the entire northern side. In earlier times various commercial activities occupied the southern side, all making use of their waterside location but by 1935 barge traffic to their quays had ceased. The truncated remains of the eighteenth-century public wharf can be seen at the head.

The south side of Springfield Basin, c.1900, when attractive granaries and warehouses lined the canal.

Another view of part of the southern side of Springfield Basin, c.1920. In the foreground is the barge *Seven Brothers* loaded with building materials. She was owned by Edward Woodcraft, a barge proprietor at Heybridge Basin.

This reproduction of an old engraving (detail) shows part of Chelmsford's original Gas Works, close to the public wharf, from where it obtained its coal supply.

A close-up of Coates Wharf, c.1955. The barge, in an undercover berth, is moored immediately next to Brown & Son's extensive timber sheds.

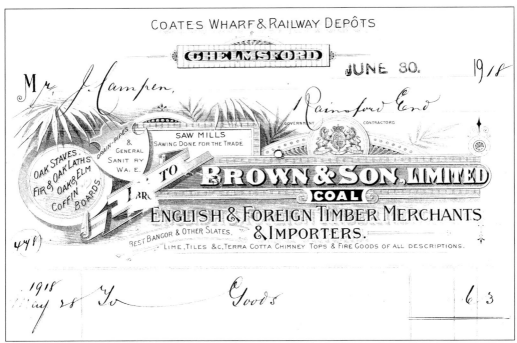

Letterhead of Brown & Son, sent in 1918 to a customer for goods purchased. At the time the firm were merchants trading throughout mid Essex in goods barged up the canal.

A view of Springfield Basin, 1955, as seen from inside the well-stocked timber sheds, when the company still barged all their imported softwood to Chelmsford.

A view of the Basin from near its head, *c*.1955. On the left are Brown & Son's timber sheds, whilst on the right are premises which earlier in the century were all served by barges. The tall building on the extreme right is the gas forming plant, built immediately after the war but demolished in the 1960s.

A motor barge approaches the timber wharf on 2 April 1960, loaded with Baltic softwood.

Springfield Basin, *c*.1975, empty of barge traffic and already showing signs of the dereliction which lasted until 1993.

Unloading timber by hand into Brown's warehouse at Coates Wharf from a motor barge, 1959. The site of the warehouse is now occupied by flats.

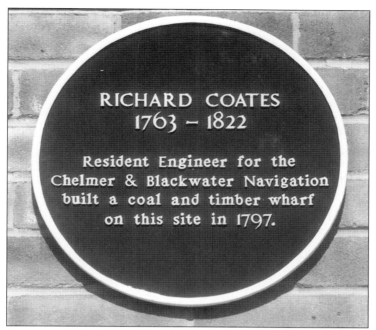

On the redevelopment of Springfield Basin this blue plaque commemorating the life and works of Richard Coates, the resident engineer in charge of constructing the Navigation, was unveiled.

Springfield Cut in 1929. An empty barge proceeds upstream towards Springfield Basin, with a bargee leading the horse along the towpath.

The last surviving Chelmer wooden barge *Susan* was captured on film at the same place in 2000, proceeding downstream to its base at the Sandford Mill Museum. Walking the towpath is Geof Bowles, Curator of the Museum.

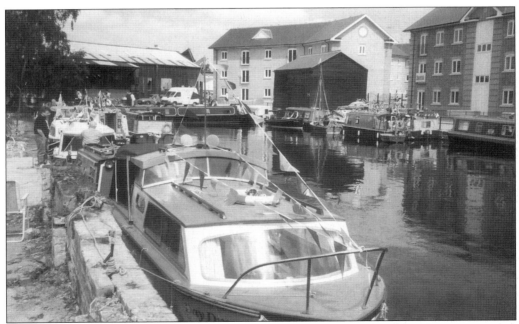

In 1993, water was returned to Springfield Basin and its approach channel and redevelopment of the quayside buildings started. In 1997, a boat rally was held to commemorate the 200th anniversary of the opening of the Basin. This picture provides a striking contrast to the same scene shown on page 20.

Springfield Basin, 2000. *Susan* approaches the old public wharf at the head of the Basin. Although some redevelopment of the southern bank has taken place several old structures still remain.

This view of modern pleasure craft moored alongside Coates Quay in 2000 makes an interesting contrast with the 1935 photograph shown on page 13, when the wharf was used solely for commercial purposes.

Susan moored snugly alongside the old public wharf at the head of the Basin. Shops and flats now stand on the old yard.

The motor barge *Jimmy* loaded with timber, approaching Hoe Mill Lock, Ulting, on its way to Chelmsford, *c.*1960.

Two
Down the Navigation

A heavily loaded timber barge approaches Bundocks Bridge, near Sandford Lock, c.1955. This is one of only five surviving arched bridges built to John Rennie's standard design on the navigation and the only one with a towpath passing under the arch.

Moulsham Mill, *c.*1905. Chelmsford was a large water and steam mill, drawing its power from both the River Can and the Chelmer before they joined the canal. For most of the nineteenth century it had a wharf, receiving coal and from where flour was shipped to Heybridge Basin, but when this picture was taken the trade had just transferred to the railway. In the 1960s, the river, as part of a flood prevention scheme was diverted away from the mill and for some years it was completely disused. Subsequently, it has been converted into a successful business and conference centre. Among the organisations now using the old mill is the Chelmsford Branch of the Inland Waterways Association, who hold their monthly social gatherings there.

Two loaded timber barges were an unusual sight passing through Springfield Lock on their way to Brown & Son's wharf on 16 August 1929. Normally the barges worked singly.

On 29 September 1993, these motor boats became two of the first vessels to pass through the newly restored lock to the Basin.

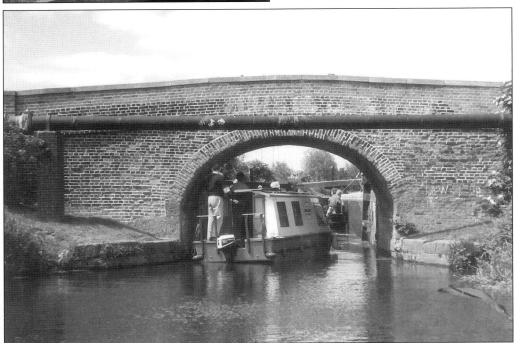

A motor cruiser passes under Springfield Lock Bridge in September 1997 to enter the lock chamber. This is the first of the John Rennie designed bridges along the navigation and it is therefore doubly unfortunate that its attractive appearance has been marred by the presence of an unsightly gas main spanning the channel.

The Chelmer Road Bridge is a short distance below Springfield Lock. This was constructed in the early 1930s as part of Chelmsford's original bypass and, unlike some of the other bridges, it has superb headroom with space for a towpath on either side. It was built to allow seasonal floods to pass unhindered downstream.

Barnes Mill, April 1960. A corn mill has existed on this site since Saxon times. In the nineteenth century the waterwheel was supplemented by a steam plant but by 1950 the latter had been dismantled and the mill only used occasionally for grinding animal feed. The stoutly constructed towpath bridge spanning the lower part of the millpond is in the foreground.

The same scene, about fifteen years later. By then the mill had been converted into a private house, sadly, losing some of its character in the process.

Recreational craft were rarely allowed to use the locks before 1973 but once a year Chelmsford Boating (now Canoe) Club were able to obtain permission for their converted pontoon to pass down to Heybridge. It is seen here, c.1955, in Barnes Lock, together with another craft, also on its way to the Basin.

A canoeist approaches Bundocks Bridge, near Sandford Lock, *c.*1955. In those days only craft able to portage around the locks were normally permitted on the waterway.

It was rarely possible for canoes and light craft to negotiate the locks but on one occasion, *c.*1960, a party of canoeists, together with several dinghy owners were allowed to pass through Sandford Lock. George King, who lived in the adjacent lock house, is seen watching the proceedings from the bank. Canoe Club member, Barry Mead, crosses the lock via the lower gates.

Sandford Lock, 1973. One of the boats taking part in the IWA Chelmsford Rally of Boats prepares to enter the chamber. Just behind is *Susan*, then in use as the Canal Company's maintenance boat.

Sandford Lock is now used regularly by pleasure craft. This large cabin cruiser passes through in summer 2000.

A narrow boat proceeding upstream to take part in the 1997 rally marking the bicentenary of the opening of the waterway. A particular feature of the canal is the almost continuous lines of bat willow planted as a crop by the Navigation Company, giving it almost the appearance of a French canal. On maturity they are destined to be made into cricket bats in Britain or Pakistan.

Another view of the boat seen on the previous page, passing through the lock. Ahead is the leafy vista of Sandford Cut, flanked by an avenue of bat willows.

On a perfect summer's day in 1929, and with little to mark its passage through the water, a barge nears Sandford Lock, with a load of Baltic timber destined for Brown & Son's wharf at Springfield Basin.

'Graces' footbridge, seen here in 1955, was first built by Richard Coates to allow pedestrian access across the canal from the parish of Springfield to Little Baddow. Here, the author (extreme left) watches canoeist, Graham Slater, pass underneath. Subsequently, the bridge has been completely rebuilt to the original appearance, maintaining the traditional navigation height.

The miller at Little Baddow made extensive use of the navigation for shipping coal to his own steam-driven roller mills and also to export flour to London and elsewhere. Sadly, in 1900, it was destroyed by fire and never rebuilt. All that remains is a small part of the mill house, now in private occupation.

Little Baddow Lock, c.1970. The channel leading from the former mill can just be glimpsed immediately to the left of the lock. Behind the lock, on land owned by the Canal Company, is a large grove of willow trees, normally felled as they reach maturity, after a period of about fifteen years.

Little Baddow Mill house, pictured here from across the large pond has been used as a private house since the fire of 1900, which destroyed both the mill and most of the house. In more recent years there have been various proposals to convert the premises into a licensed restaurant but its future remains uncertain. The tail of the lock can be seen in the foreground.

The Black Bridge, c.1930, was probably one of the original bridges built by Richard Coates. Unlike the substantial arched structures elsewhere along the canal, only the abutments were of brick, the centre span being wooden. By 1950 it was rickety and unsafe. Although the replacement is made entirely of reinforced concrete, superficially it has the appearance of being of wooden construction, complete with open side rails, so maintaining a traditional appearance, which is entirely appropriate to the locality's Conservation Area status. It now carries substantial morning and evening rush hour traffic.

The replacement Black Bridge. Unfortunately, like the earlier structure, the current headroom at 6ft, is barely adequate and when water levels are high there are problems for craft like *Victoria* to pass beneath. In hindsight it is a great pity that the opportunity was not taken, on rebuilding, to raise the headroom.

The Chelmsford Boating (now Canoe) Club's pontoon houseboat passing through Little Baddow Lock, *c.*1955. David Eade, then Hon. Secretary, stands on the fore deck. The small brick building behind the lock gate is the former 'bothy', or bunkhouse, where the bargees could sleep overnight. The black wooden building is used for storing maintenance equipment.

The former 'bothy' at Little Baddow as seen in April 1960. In the 1970s it was renovated and converted into the Navigation Company's office. More recently an extension has been added.

After barge traffic ceased in the early 1970s the waterway was opened to pleasure craft and, with assistance from the Chelmsford Branch of the Inland Waterways Association, a boat slip was built aiding the development of the immediate locality as moorings for private craft.

A maintenance barge proceeds downstream from Paper Mill Lock, c.1910, carrying a new lock gate for installation lower down the waterway. It was – and is – normal company practice to build new gates at Paper Mills and transport them by water to the required location.

The next lock, Rushes, is set in extremely pleasant, quiet, open countryside remote from roads and, on a warm summer's day, it is a favourite spot for swimmers and sunbathers. As *Victoria*, c.1980, quits the chamber, after locking through, there is already a rush by swimmers to resume their dip.

For most of the way between Chelmsford and Heybridge Basin few waterside buildings are to be seen. An attractive exception is Ulting Parish Church, which provides a popular venue for visiting craft.

In 1970, shortly before barge traffic ceased, the Inland Waterways Association were able to hire a motor barge for a members' trip along the entire canal. The boat is seen here passing through Rushes Lock. About seventy people were on board.

An empty barge makes its way upstream towards Beeleigh Lock skirting Beeleigh Weir, c.1900, the latter spanned by the long towpath bridge in the centre of the picture. It is here that the Chelmer meets the Blackwater. Water from the latter flows over the weir. An artificial channel then proceeds beyond the weir to Heybridge Basin.

The entrance into the Long Pond – as the artificial channel is called – is barred by two pairs of gates, known as Beeleigh Flood Gates, normally unused, except in times of flood. Here, c.1955, the author crawls along the balance beam to unfasten the padlocked gates so that a party of canoeists may paddle through.

Three
Heybridge Basin
and the Long Pond

Heybridge Basin, *c.*1890, with a sailing vessel moored upstream from the lock. Facing, on the right of the picture, is the Old Ship pub, once known as the Chelmer Brig, with a row of cottages and shops adjoining. Behind the boat a timber framed building can be spotted. This was used for many years as a granary, a temporary store for exported corn and flour.

This section from an nineteenth-century map shows Heybridge Basin and the adjacent little community, when it was virtually isolated by land from Maldon. Most of the villagers were employed either directly or indirectly on the canal. Many were descendants of the navvies who came with Richard Coates from Suffolk to build the waterway.

The junction of Long Pond with Langford Cut (right), which led to Langford Mill, c.1905. On the left is the entrance to Beeleigh Flood Gates. The cut was extensively used to carry flour from the mill to Heybridge Basin, with coal as a return cargo until the latter part of the nineteenth century. However, by the turn of the last century, the trade had already transferred to rail and the cut disused. Even today, though, the channel holds water.

Langford Mill, c.1900, at the head of the cut, was a large timber-framed flour mill, burnt down in 1879 and subsequently replaced with the present handsome brick structure. In the 1920s, it was converted into an abstraction point for the Water Company, with water pumped to their newly built Langford Works.

The Long Pond, looking towards Heybridge, from the tail of Beeleigh Flood Gates, *c*.1910. The marshes on the right have since been converted into a popular golf club.

The first part of the Long Pond to Heybridge village incorporates a minor channel of the River Blackwater, which flows to the mill at the head of Heybridge Creek. Heybridge Mill was an attractive Grade l listed building. Sadly, it was demolished in 1955, when the creek was stanked off and infilled. The Lond Pond continues for a further mile or so to Heybridge Basin as a completely artificial channel.

From Beeleigh to Heybridge Basin the Long Pond passes through land increasingly liable to sea water flooding, a result of global warming. In consequence, about 1990, the Environment Agency built this set of stop boards midway to the Basin. They are only intended to come into use when there is danger from a tidal surge.

At the approach to Maldon the canal was bridged twice by the branch railway to the town. One of the crossings is seen here, c.1910. In the 1980s a town bypass was constructed along the railway alignment and the bridge replaced by the present structure, fortunately with navigation headroom.

Maldon is expanding and land next to the canal is rapidly being developed. One of the recent buildings is Tesco, built on land previously used by the Navigation Company to deposit dredgings. The store has been designed to have a superficial resemblance to the exterior of a Victorian railway station. It is now a popular shopping point for boaters.

This fascinating aerial picture of Heybridge Basin, c.1965 shows the original 1793 lock gates, together with a later lock extension, built to allow the passage of brigs, which enabled modern coasters to enter the enclosed water. Immediately upstream are a number of eel containers and in the 1950s and 1960s there was a thriving trade in live eels imported into the Basin for the London market. The line of moored craft on the left bank are seagoing yachts and cruisers which then – as now – use the canal as a freshwater haven.

Heybridge Basin c.1955. The eels were removed from their containers by nets, weighed, crated and sent daily to London. The eels were imported from Northern Europe. This trade has subsequently been discontinued and replaced by the importation of frozen eels from North America.

Heybridge Basin, *c.*1955. The still water of the Basin is a popular venue for angling.

Heybridge Basin, *c.*1900. A large three-masted sailing boat is moored in the basin, whilst a 'Stackie' waits to depart. In the bottom of the picture an empty canal barge awaits a load.

After Heybridge Basin Lock was lengthened in the early 1960s coasters regularly entered the Basin. Here, in September 1965, loose timber is being unloaded into motor barges from MV *Wergan*, prior to proceeding to Chelmsford.

Heybridge Basin, together with the lower part of the Long Pond have been extensively used as freshwater mooring since early in the twentieth century. This was the scene in 1933. Over the years the numbers and size of craft making use of the facilities have fluctuated, to reach a peak in the 1960s.

Heybridge Basin, *c.*1955. Before the lock was lengthened coasters were unable to enter the Basin and normal practice was to unload cargoes into dismasted Thames barges near Osea Island. They were then towed to the Basin and cargo was loaded into canal barges before journeying on to Chelmsford. After the lock chamber was lengthened the coasters entered the Basin and unloaded directly for Chelmsford.

Today, although there are less craft permanently moored at the Basin than in earlier years, it still remains popular, particularly by visiting yachtsmen.

Following the demise of the timber trade in 1972, the basin is used infrequently by large craft, although it remains possible for them to enter. In 1998, this former whaler, *Ocean Defender*, owned by an environmental group, put into the port.

An interior view of the massive lock, built to take vessels up to 107ft long, 26ft beam and drawing 12ft of water. The original entrance is marked by the rounded stonework. The 1960s extension allowed larger craft to enter.

This unusual picture taken from the estuary shows a sailing vessel entering the Basin on the rising tide, c.1910.

Four
Above the Navigation

The 1797 Act authorising the construction of the waterway allowed for the head of the canal to be either in Chelmsford or Springfield parishes, but due to problems with the Mildmay entail, which affected the whole of Chelmsford, it was decided to build the terminus in Springfield. Nevertheless, despite the lack of a statutory right of navigation, the River Can above the legal limit is an attractive – and very well used – area for boating and canoeing. In 1987, this party of local canoeists were filmed paddling under New London Road Bridge. Currently there is a proposal to construct a linking channel between the canal and the River Chelmer, which would allow larger craft to cruise through to Central Park and beyond.

In the 1960s, the Rivers Chelmer and Can were both widened and deepened through Chelmsford town centre as part of a flood prevention scheme. In retaining the traditional water levels massive sluices were built downstream of the main built up area. Although, enthusiasts at the time requested that a lock should be included within the scheme, which would have enabled boats, for the first time, to pass into the main area of Chelmsford, this idea was not accepted by the then Essex River Authority. However, at the request of the IWA, the local council persuaded the latter to build a boat roller path alongside the sluices. This allows light craft to safely bypass them. For over forty years this has been a very welcome and well-used facility, used by hundreds of paddlers annually.

Had the original proposal to terminate the waterway at Moulsham Bridge been followed, this scene, c.1900, would have been very different. Instead of just a few moored rowing boats, the waterside would have been alive with cargo barges.

A more recent view of Moulsham Bridge on the River Can. This structure, built in the eighteenth century, is now a scheduled ancient monument. Fortunately, the headroom is more than adequate for boats of *Victoria*'s size to pass beneath if navigation is extended to this stretch.

Boating has been taken place for over 100 years on the River Can above the Kings Head Meadow Sluices. Many people believe that a public right of navigation has been acquired. In the 1950s and 1960s, it was regular practice to formally exercise this right at least once a year. In this picture, *c.*1955, various types of craft are seen passing in convoy under one of Central Park's footbridges.

This striking picture shows the River Can as it passes under the railway viaduct just upstream from Central Park. If a connection is eventually made between the canal, the River Can and the Chelmer, the upper limit for larger craft would probably be at this point, although smaller craft would be able to venture a further half a mile or so.

The River Can viewed from Waterhouse Lane Bridge, c.1970, a few years after the completion of the flood prevention scheme. More recently, vegetation has grown along the banks reducing the effective width of the channel, but, nevertheless, it remains well used by local paddlers.

Since the completion of the flood prevention scheme, Chelmsford town centre has seen much redevelopment, including an inner relief road. The associated bridge over the River Can is pictured here, Fortunately, both this and the one over the Chelmer, have been built to full navigation height.

Recent development schemes in Chelmsford have featured the canal and rivers, and created footpaths alongside them. At The Meadows, a small esplanade with steps down to the water is already built to receive canal craft, which, sadly, will only arrive once a connection has been made to the canal. It is, however, most unfortunate that, owing to a mistake not spotted by the borough planners when the redevelopment scheme was under consideration, a number of footbridges were constructed with limited headroom. They need to be raised if larger craft are to be encouraged.

The River Can in 2000, upstream from the town centre. The attractively landscaped Central Park is on the right bank, with modern office development on the left. The addition of narrow boats would enliven the scene.

Five

Restoration & Maintenance

In 1993, the IWA Chelmsford Branch carried out the complete restoration of Springfield Lock, together with the approach channel to Springfield Basin. Work to the lock necessitated the demolition of the chamber walls and rebuilding.

Prior to restoration work, the upper part of the canal was totally derelict, the lock unusable and the approach channel choked by bulrushes, as seen here in 1985.

Restoration work commenced in 1992. The IWA adopted a high profile, winning the confidence of the Chelmsford Borough Council, who loaned them a large brick shed, in which they were able to store their equipment, alongside the cut.

The same site when restoration was completed in 1993. Concurrently with rebuilding the lock, the Rennie-designed bridge was repointed, missing coping stones replaced and brickwork cleaned.

The whole of Springfield Cut and the Basin area was dredged by mechanical digger, probably the first time since the canal was opened in 1797.

The same scene in 1997, the cut restored to its original appearance, although the type and size of craft had completely changed. In 1797 the procession of boats queuing to enter the Basin were all 60ft long by 16ft loaded barges, rather than the small motor cruisers and narrow boats now found on the waterway.

Springfield Lock early in 1993 whilst still being restored. The chamber walls are in process of being rebuilt and new gates are in course of installation, minus their balance beams and paddles. The dredged Springfield Cut, newly restored to water, stretches into the distance towards the Basin.

Springfield Lock, prior to restoration, 1992. The upper gates were in poor condition. One of the lower gates had completely collapsed and the chamber badly silted. When filmed, dredging had already taken place to the approach channel.

The same scene in September 1997, following the reopening of the lock in 1993, with a variety of recreational craft locking through.

Above: Shire horses at Gernon Bushes, near Epping, pull oak timber intended for the replacement gates. The trees were obtained by the IWA, and members, using only hand tools, cut the timber into planks and beams. It was brought to Chelmsford for assembly.

Right: The new gates were manufactured on site. Here, a carpenter is making one of the massive mortise joints which hold the balance beams to the lock frame.

The carcass of one of the new upper gates, with the iron strengthening straps fitted, and the balance beam and paddles still to be installed. The final task is to apply bitumen.

John Gale, of Chelmsford IWA, takes a well earned cat nap during the restoration work in 1993, between carrying loads of dredgings in his dumper truck. Much of the material contained toxic waste and was removed to a licensed tip.

In March 1992, prior to restoration Springfield Basin was a shallow and unsightly stretch of water surrounded by derelict and unused warehouse buildings.

The restored Springfield Basin, 1997, when a boat rally was held to celebrate the 200th anniversary of the opening of the waterway. Rehabilitation of the Basin was the catalyst for the renewal and redevelopment of the surrounding area. Since this picture was taken, further bankside building works have taken place.

Concurrent with the other restoration work, the feeder channel to the Basin was also cleared of debris. The route – partly piped – snakes its way from the River Chelmer to the basin head. As the channel is the Basin's sole source of water supply, the removal of 200 years of accumulated rubbish was of prime importance.

The open section of the feeder channel is brick enclosed. Due to lack of maintenance the water flow had, over the years, been reduced to a mere trickle and, until cleared out, was inadequate to supply a proper supply of water for lockage.

Clearance of the channel took several weeks and the removal of the mud and silt was a very dirty job but, as a result, an adequate flow of water to the basin was restored. Subsequently, a multi-storey car park has been built on the far side of the channel, with a surface car park on the near side. The open channel has been incorporated into the new development as a local feature.

Maintenance by the Canal Company always involves the unexpected! Shopping trolleys are now quite commonly retrieved. Rarely, however, are they called upon to deal with abandoned cars. The photographer was on hand, *c*.1965, to record efforts by several of Brown's employees to retrieve a sunken car blocking the channel.

Eventually a line was passed through the car and it was towed by the barge *Anne* to the bank for disposal. This difficult operation was only achieved with the huge Harbourmaster engine operating at full power.

At least one pair of lock gates are normally replaced each year and the method of construction has changed little since 1793. In 1950, Harry Gowers, canal employee, was pictured at work, with mallet and chisel on the new gate at Paper Mill.

Repairs to the lock chamber are normally carried out concurrently with the fitting of new gates and the accumulated debris removed from the floor. This picture, taken in May 1982, shows the cill under repair at Sandford Lock.

Before any lock repair or maintenance work can be carried out a temporary dam must be built above and below the chamber and the water moved. In the past these dams tended to be rather makeshift wooden structures with planks driven vertically into the canal bed behind a stout cross beam and made watertight by tarpaulins, sealed with puddled clay. Today, dams are often of heavy gauge plastic sheeting backed by a timber frame. In this picture, c.1955, a simple pile driver is hammering baulks of timber into the canal bed. Bill Siggers, the canal foreman is back to the camera. Second on the left is George King, with his usual cheerful smile.

Work on the, massive frame of the new gate at Paper Mill, c.1955, with virtually all the company's manual employees at work. To the left, Bill Siggers, is wielding a hammer and chisel, whilst on the right, George King appears to be drilling holes prior to fitting ironwork.

A new gate, at Paper Mill Lock, Little Baddow, *c*.1955, ready to be craned into position. The balance beams, together with the paddles, will be fitted when both gates are in position and strapped to the lock wall.

The present dredger at Paper Mill Lock, *c*.2000. It is mounted on the same flat as the earlier machine.

In 1948, the canal suffered a massive breach at Beeleigh Weir, the result of exceptional winter floods. For a time, there seemed to be a possibility that the canal might be abandoned but eventually several old barges were successfully manoeuvred into the breach and sunk and a new embankment constructed around them.

The waterway reopened for traffic in 1950 and the first load of timber is seen passing the site of the breach, which had just been infilled with newly piled sheet steel and 'back filled' with concrete.

As the waterway is actually a navigable river, dredging is a regular activity along its entire length. Normal practice is to heap the spoil on the adjacent bank, where it will slowly compact down. The Navigation Company's diesel Priestman dredger is seen here near Stonhams Lock,

c.1955, with George King at the controls. It was reputed to be somewhat temperamental in behaviour and George the only person able to operate it properly. It has since been replaced by a hydraulic machine.

In 1998, the bypass weir at Ricketts Lock suddenly collapsed, resulting in the complete loss of water on the Hoe Mill stretch. On examination it was found that the entire weir had been built above an elm log base, which had disintegrated after 200 years of service. The weir has since been totally rebuilt, using modern materials. However, it has been made as a visual replica of the original Rennie- designed structure.

The whole of the Chelmer & Blackwater Navigation was declared a linear Conservation Area, c.1990. In 1998, it was awarded a substantial grant via a Conservation Area Partnership Scheme, from the local authorities and the National Heritage Lottery Fund. This has enabled many of the locks, weirs and other installations to be repaired or renovated to a very high standard. In 2000, repointing of the Rennie-designed bridge at Beeleigh was carried out, using lime mortar to the original formula.

In 1999, major renovations were carried out to Little Baddow Lock with funds provided via the Conservation Area Partnership (CAPS). Works included repairs to the chamber walls, including repointing and installation of two new pairs of gates. For the first time, an escape ladder was inserted into the lock wall in a somewhat belated recognition that this safety feature is needed now that the locks are predominantly used by small privately owned motor boats, usually crewed by husband and wife teams.

The Navigation's maintenance barge *Julie* was originally one of Brown & Son's timber barges and was acquired by the company when the former ceased using the canal in 1972. Now an essential part of the company's maintenance equipment with her huge bulk she is able to move large quantities of equipment and materials to any required waterside location.

In 2001, work started on a small marina on part of an old scrapyard. This important new facility is immediately above Springfield Lock and will provide safe moorings for about twelve boats and is being built concurrently with new flats on the adjoining land. The entrance to the marina is pictured here a few weeks after development started.

Six
Some Navigation Personalities

The Chelmer & Blackwater Navigation was designed by the famous canal engineer, John Rennie (1761-1821), and based on a survey by Charles Wedge. His trusted assistant was Richard Coates. Although Rennie kept tight control of the work, he is reputed to have only visited the waterway five times.

Richard Coates, a civil engineer from Yorkshire, was in day-to-day charge of the canal construction. After it opened in 1797, he settled in Springfield and became an import and export merchant, with a fleet of barges. Sadly, no portrait of him seems to have survived. He died in 1822, only a year after John Rennie, and is buried in All Saints Churchyard, Springfield, in an impressive tomb. His family were also laid to rest beside him.

As a successful businessman, Richard Coates, became a major local benefactor, providing large donations to charities. He was one of the first governors of Springfield National School (now The Bishops School) and later paid for the construction of two additional wings. He also provided funds towards restoration work at All Saints Church, Springfield.

George Cliff, the yard foreman for Richard Coates, eventually became the owner of the coal and timber business at Springfield Wharf. On his death the firm passed to James Brown and became Brown & Son. This portrait of George at the quayside remained in the boardroom until the firm was taken over by Travis Perkins.

The late Col. John Cramphorn T. D., was Chairman of the Company of Proprietors of the Chelmer & Blackwater Navigation for nearly thirty years. During that time he steered the company from its transport roots into the leisure sector. He is seen here on board *Victoria*, *c*. 1990.

The popular and ever cheerful George King spent most of his working life on the navigation as lock keeper, dredger man and then as foreman. He is seen here opening a lock paddle, c.1955.

Eddie Webb is another familiar long-standing employee of the navigation, proving himself versatile in carrying out many essential functions, from maintenance to skippering *Victoria*. He is pictured here steering the vessel from Springfield Lock during the celebrations marking the 1993 anniversary of the founding of the Navigation Company.

Former Company Secretary and current Director, Bill Spall, with his wife at the Navigation Company's bicentenary cruise in 1993.

Col. Cramphorn (centre) with Eddie Webb (left) and Francis F. Stunt (right), then Secretary of the Navigation Company, on the fore deck of *Victoria* at its launch at Heybridge Basin in 1973.

Left: King John's wife, Queen Eleanor (otherwise Mrs Judith Abbott of Blackwater Boats), with windlass on board *Susan* at Springfield Lock in September 1999, when Chelmsford was celebrating the 800th anniversary of the town charter granted by King John in 1199.

Below: Chelmsford Duchess led by the late Reg Spalding, a well-known local farmer, tows the narrow boat *Rennie* along the River Chelmer in 1977 in celebration of the 180th anniversary of the opening of the navigation.

Four canal employees pause from their work of cill replacement at Sandford Lock, June 1951. George King is second from left, with Bill Siggers, the canal foreman, second from the right.

A popular pastime for youngsters in the summer months was to 'bag' a lift on a barge to and from Heybridge. Here, *c.*1955, the boys are obviously thoroughly enjoying their free day out.

Seven

Boats on the Navigation

A barge at Sandford Lock, c.1950, typical of those on the Navigation from 1797 until their replacement in post-war years by motor boats. Their similarity to Thames barges can clearly be seen. They normally remained in service for very many years due to their stout construction.

The directors of the Navigation Company making their annual inspection of the line, c.1950, using a barge borrowed from Brown & Son, the timber merchants. The vessel was thoroughly cleaned out, sheeted over and provided with seats and tables. During the course of the day an excellent luncheon was provided for the directors and their guests. Fred Hoy is seen leading the barge horse, Chelmsford Duke.

A horse-drawn barge approaches Springfield Lock, c.1950, with a load of timber. When full, the boats carried 25 tons.

Two empty motor barges passing under Paper Mill Lock, Little Baddow, c.1960, on their way to Heybridge to load tirnber. Their power units were large 'Harbourmaster' diesel outboard engines and the boats carried up to 40 tons of cargo.

It was occasionally possible for organisations to hire a barge for the day. Here, at Rushes Lock, *c*.1970, some seventy IWA members were blessed with good weather as they enjoyed a trip from Chelmsford to Heybridge Basin.

This large motor barge propeller was photographed *c.*1965 whilst the boat was passing through one of the locks.

This picture of *Julie* the last of the Chelmer steel motor barges was captured on film in 1997 at the Navigation Company's operational headquarters at Paper Mill Lock. She is now used solely for maintenance purposes.

The canal company's boat *Victoria* under construction at Bingley in 1975. Col. John Cramphom, chairman of the company stands on the foredeck, with two of the boat builders.

Victoria being craned into the canal at Heybridge Basin in 1975.

In the 1980s, a newly formed company, Blackwater Boats, introduced a small fleet of four-berth narrow boats to the waterway. Here, the first vessel is craned into Sandford Cut, where the company have established their hire base. The company specialise in short break holidays and has clients from all over the world, who are attracted by the peaceful, unspoilt charm of the Chelmer.

Blackwater Boats' small fleet of hire narrow boats moored at their base at Sandford Lock, Springfield in 1993.

In Victorian times trips were extremely popular for church and school parties, with owners willing to loan a boat for the day. The town's famous photographer, Fred Spalding, was on hand to record for posterity an event in July 1899, with the passengers all dressed in their Sunday finery, passing through Springfield Lock in their attractively decorated vessel.

Current problems caused by the accidental introduction of American Pennywort to the entire waterway and its rampant growth have resulted in the Navigation Company purchasing a weed cutter. 'Berky' removes the worst of the weed but does not solve an ongoing problem, for which a solution still needs to be found.

A variety of privately owned powered craft are now to be found on the waterway. At present most are petrol-driven but steam-powered craft have made their appearance within recent years. This elegant vessel, the *Araminta*, was photographed in 1998 near its base at Paper Mill Lock.

Next page: The company's Priestman Dredger is seen here moored at Treasure Island, Paper Mill Lock, *c.*1965.

Locking into Heybridge Basin, c.1960, the motor vessel *Mutua-Fides*, with a cargo of sawn timber destined for Brown & Son at Chelmsford. She was one of the largest vessels to enter its enclosed waters.

The Navigation Company's charter barge *Victoria* near Paper Mill, *c.*1978, cruising towards Rushes Lock. This popular vessel is 58ft long by 12ft 6ins wide and, when loaded, has a draft of 2ft 9ins. Weighing 30 tons unladen, she is licensed to carry forty-eight passengers. Apart from the forward open observation deck, she is completely enclosed. She is chartered for a variety of functions, from wedding receptions and parties to business conventions and school outings.

Canoeing is extremely popular on the waterway and Chelmsford Canoe Club is one of the largest clubs in Eastern England. For over fifty years it has organised an annual canoe race of up to fourteen miles along the canal. Normally, up to 100 paddlers take part. These paddlers in double seater canoes, c.1960, are lining up for the start of one of the classes beneath the Chelmer Road bridge. The winners were R. Fish and B. Smith (centre) from the London-based Canoe Touring Club.

K. Pereira of Twickenham Canoe Club, seen here approaching the finish at Heybridge Basin, was the winner of the single seater class in the annual Chelmer Canoe Race, c.1960.

Eight

Notable Events

Bill Spall (left), then Secretary of the Navigation and Director, and William Marriage (no relation to author) (right), together with their wives, about to take part in the company's celebratory cruise on the waterway in 1993 marking the 200th anniversary of the founding of the company.

For several years in the late 1950s, the IWA were able to organise a day trip along the waterway, starting from Moulsham Mill, Chelmsford and finishing at Heybridge Basin. Fred Hoy leads Chelmsford Duke, whilst the author (and organiser of the event) walked alongside as the boat approaches Chelmer Road Bridge.

After the introduction of motor barges to the waterway, the IWA were again able to hold several trips along the canal. In this picture, c.1968, the boat containing about seventy members passes Beeleigh Weir.

Left: Since 1793, when the Navigation Company was formed, an annual meeting has been held. Originally, they met at the Black Boy pub in Chelmsford, but nowadays, meetings are held at their office at Paper Mill lock.

Below: The Company of Proprietors of the Chelmer & Blackwater Navigation Ltd hold an annual inspection of the line, unique to this particular waterway. Until *Victoria* became available for use, an ordinary working boat was used, cleaned out and sheeted over for the day, with chairs and tables added. Chelmsford Duke, led by Fred Hoy, is towing the inspection barge passing Barnes Mill, *c.*1950.

After the construction of the canal in 1797 a small community grew up around Heybridge Basin with poor road communications to the outside world. In the event of a death in the village it was customary for the coffin and funeral party to be barged to Heybridge cemetery.

In 1973, following the news that commercial traffic had ceased on the Chelmer, the London & Home Counties Branch of the IWA decided to hold a Rally of Boats at Chelmsford to promote the canal for recreational use. The barge *Susan*, then in use as a maintenance boat, was pressed into service for public trips which were very popular. Passengers are waiting to board below Kings Head Sluices.

At the time there were no boats other than canoes on the waterway and enthusiasts brought their craft from elsewhere. Many came on trailers, whilst others entered the canal from the estuary. This four-berth motor cruiser, owned by Rally Chairman, Maurice Frost, was trailed from the River Stort and lifted into Springfield Cut.

Motor boats and their happy crews gather for the photographer to record the 1973 Chelmsford Rally of Boats, which successfully kick-started the present use of the navigation for recreational craft.

Rennie towed by Chelmsford Duchess starts the return journey from Kings Head Meadow to its base at Paper Mill Lock.

In 1977, the newly formed IWA Chelmsford Branch marked the 180th anniversary of the opening of the navigation with a cruise to Kings Head Meadow on the River Chelmer. The narrow boat *Rennie* carrying Chelmsford Carnival Queen and the Chairman of the Branch, Gerry Parker, was welcomed by a Sea Cadet guard of honour. Several canadian canoes accompanied *Rennie*.

In 1988, a Water Festival was held to mark the centenary of Chelmsford as a borough. The IWA contribution was a well-attended Rally of Boats at Kings Head Meadow. Scores of boats came and *Victoria* made a series of short public trips. She is seen here with a full complement of passengers.

Among those attending the 1988 rally was Charles Stock in his boat *Shoal Waters*, which sailed the whole fourteen miles up from the Blackwater estuary.

In Spring 1993, the IWA Chelmsford Branch, who organised and carried out the restoration of Springfield Cut and Basin held a rally of boats to celebrate the reopening to coincide with the 200th anniversary of the passing of the Chelmer Navigation Act. *Victoria* led the cavalcade of boats along the restored pound. This picture was taken whilst she was still in the lock chamber.

Until 2000, Henry Marriage (no relation to author) was Chairman of the Company, shown here in Victorian cutaway, bow tie and bowler at the Company's own celebration of the bicentenary in summer 1993. He successfully steered the company firmly into the twenty-first century.

The headquarters of the 1993 rally was in King Head Meadow, from where public trips in *Victoria* took place. The Mayor of Chelmsford, Cllr Christopher Kingsley, and his wife were two of the visiting dignitaries.

Victoria at Kings Head Meadow, the 1993 rally site.

In 1997, the Friends of the Chelmer & Blackwater Navigation (now Chelmer Canal Trust) held a rally commemorating the bicentenary of the opening of the canal. In May 1797, a small fleet of decorated barges entered the Basin, greeted by cheering townsfolk and playing bands. In an echo of that event, *Susan*, with a cavalcade of boats, slowly enters the Basin.

The view from *Susan* leaving Springfield Lock. Ahead, a variety of boats wait to join the procession.

The 1997 cavalcade of boats viewed from *Susan*, as they approach Springfield Basin, with the steam yacht, *Aramima*, following and other vessels behind.

117

A small fleet of visiting narrow boats moor alongside a derelict wharf near the head of the Basin, 1997. A granary previously stood on the site, but more recently the land was used as a builders' store. An Italian-themed restaurant now stands there.

When barge traffic declined, the public wharf at the head of the Basin ceased to be used and only Coates Wharf, on the north side, continued in trade. The first barge to revisit the public wharf for about 100 years was *Susan*, here moored snugly alongside, 1997.

118

Nine
The Motor Barge *Susan*

Susan is the very last of the traditional wooden barges, which from 1797 plied up and down the navigation between Springfield Basin, Chelmsford and Heybridge Basin, Maldon, carrying a variety of cargoes in open holds. *Susan*, built in 1953, varied little from the original horse-drawn vessels, although now with an diesel inboard engine. Now owned by Chelmsford Museum Service, she makes regular demonstration cruises along the navigation.

Susan was built for Brown & Son, but after they brought a small fleet of steel motor barges into use in the late 1950s, she was transferred to the Navigation Company to become a maintenance boat. At Paper Mill Lock in the early 1970s she is seen moored besides the company's dredger. Later the IWA acquired her and subsequently transferred her to a specially formed group – the Chelmer Lighter Preservation Society.

Right: Susan in her role as the company's inspection barge, *c.*1960, passing Beeleigh Weir.

Below: For several years, whilst in the ownership of the Navigation Company, *Susan*, suitably sheeted over and provided with seats, was used to take the directors on their annual inspection of the line. It was shortly after one of these occasions and, with tarpaulins still in position, she became the star of the first ever rally of boats in 1973, when she took hundreds of people on short trips along the canal from a temporary stage in Kings Head Meadow.

The Chelmer Lighter Preservation Society co-operated closely with the former Passmore Edwards Museum, of Stratford, E15, who owned several traditional Essex vessels. In this picture, c.1975, a sample cargo brought from London to Maldon by their sailing barge *Dawn* is transferred to *Susan* to be taken to Chelmsford. Jim Tildersley, then Deputy Curator of the Museum (right) watches as the author transfers a sample box. Due to increasing problems of maintenance the Museum later took over ownership of *Susan*, with the Society continuing as crew.

In 1984, funds were given by a Newham lottery to the Passmore Edwards Museum for use on *Susan*. Consequently, she motored down to Heybridge Basin and was taken to Cookes Boatyard at The Hythe, Maldon, and major repairs started. She was beached and the rotten timbers were removed and replaced. The picture shows the boat's early restoration stage.

Whilst repairs were underway, the huge propeller, located within its tunnel, could be viewed from the stern of the boat.

Repairs were completed in 1987 and *Susan* was ceremonially handed back to the museum in September of that year. This photograph shows her sitting on the barge blocks at The Hythe, with restoration work complete and sporting a fresh coat of paint and bitumen. In 1989, further work was carried out to the transom.

In 1991, following a change of policy, the Passmore Edwards Museum disposed of their small fleet of Essex craft. *Susan* was transferred to the Chelmsford Museum Service, who returned her to the town and provided moorings in the mill race at Sandford Mill. Since then, members of the Chelmer Lighter Preservation Society have assisted in its maintenance and provided crew when required. David Goodridge, seen here in 1998, is working on the Thorneycroft diesel engine.

Although the engine is very reliable it often requires two or three people to start. David Goodridge is operating the controls, whilst Steve Norton cranks the engine. A third member stands by ready to help, June 2001.

Although much of the timber was renewed in 1984, replacement is a regular feature of owning a barge. Here, in 1998, Mike Slater is scarfing in a short piece of board to replace a rotten section of the gunnel.

Geof Bowles of the Sandford Mill Museum, together with members of the Society, at work in 1993, lifting floorboards prior to maintenance.

The barge's floorboards were removed to the dry interior of the museum, where Steve Norton applies a coat of bitumen.

As is often the case with wooden boats moored on freshwater, 'gribble' has attacked the boat, damaging the bottom and the chines. In November 1997, worm repellent was applied. The unlucky worker was Dave Goodridge.

When at events Susan normally carries a token cargo to give the public some idea of the range of goods carried along the waterway. Typical cargoes shown include timber, coal, flour, bricks, slate and lime.

A view of *Susan* cruising the Chelmer near home base at Sandford Mill in 1999, with crew members of the Chelmer Lighter Preservation Society. As a result of continuing dedicated work by volunteers, the old boat remains a splendid and evocative reminder of the past importance of barge traffic to and from Chelmsford.

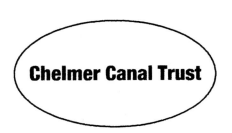

Chelmer Canal Trust

In 1996 a number of enthusiasts, with an appreciation of the special value of the Chelmer & Blackwater Navigation, formed the Friends of the Chelmer & Blackwater Navigation. Their aim was to ensure that the beautiful little waterway would be preserved, cherished and enhanced for everyone's benefit.

In 2000, in order to have a distinct identity from the still thriving Chelmer & Blackwater Navigation Company, which built the canal just over 200 years ago, the Friends changed their name to the Chelmer Canal Trust Ltd, becoming at the same time a registered charitable company, limited by guarantee. Its aims remain to preserve the waterway from Chelmsford to the sea and to promote its quality and uniqueness for public enjoyment. The Trust also became a corporate member of the IWA and the East Anglian Waterways Association.

The Trust provides a forum for the assembly and focus of views from all interested parties. It organises boating rallies, lectures, socials, historical and environmental visits, together with member cruises, as well as publishing a quarterly journal, *Coates Cuttings*. The Trust campaigns for the increased use of the waterway for boaters and other recreational users; the removal of intrusive weed; the creation of a new navigable route to the Museum of Power at Langford, via the River Blackwater; and the construction of a navigable !ink between Springfield Basin and the River Chelmer at Chelmsford.

New members are welcome. Further details can be obtained from the Hon. Secretary, 16 Roots Lane, Wickham Bishops CM8 3LS or from the Trust's web site on: www.wmv.dircon.co.uk/cct/cct.htm.

Appendix

To operate or have any form of boat on the navigation, the consent of the Chelmer & Blackwater Navigation is required. Moorings, if appropriate, also need to be arranged. The company can be contacted at Paper Mill Lock, North Hill, Little Baddow, Chelmsford, Essex CM3 4TQ. Telephone no. 01245 222025. Further details can be found on www.cbn.co.uk. Other useful addresses:

Blackwater Boats, Bumble Bee Cottage, Boxted Road, Colchester CO4 5HF Telephone no. 01206 853282

Chelmer Lighter Preservation Society, c/o 28 Goldlay Avenue, Chelmsford, Essex CM2 0TN

Chelmsford Canoe Club, Kings Head Meadow, Wharf Road, Chelmsford, Essex CM2 6LT

Inland Waterways Association, 3 Norfolk Court, Norfolk Road, Rickmansworth WD3 1LT Website: www.waterways.org.uk

Acknowledgements

The photographs and illustrations appear by kind permission of the following: Eric Boesch, David Cannon, Roy Chandler, Chelmsford Borough Council, Dudley Courtman, Brian Horsley, Tony Hoy, William Marriage and Paul Skeet. Others are from the author's own collection. I also acknowledge the help given to me by my wife, Marion, who cheerfully corrected grammatical errors and made many invaluable suggestions as to the content.